Seriya

Seriya

By

Abdul-Rasheed Na'Allah

malthouse ⋋𝓅

Malthouse Press Limited

Lagos, Benin, Ibadan, Jos, Port-Harcourt, Zaria

3

Published in Nigeria by

Malthouse Press Limited
43 Onitana Street, Off Stadium Hotel Road,
Off Western Avenue, Lagos Mainland
E-mail: malthouselagos@gmail.com
Tel: +234 802 600 3203

Distributors
African Books Collective Ltd
Email: abc@africanbookscollective.com
Website: http://www.africanbookscollective.com

4

For

My Extended Family, the Muhammadu Jimoh Golu posterities, offsprings of Ayinla Opo Manlewa Majaalekan!

Acknowledgements

My gratitude goes to my family, friends and colleagues for their solid support. To John Kinsella, Australian writer, who actually made me write this play when he asked for another play after reading my "Baba Omokewu" manuscript, and to Erica Potterbaum, who read every Act of "Seriya" before I wrote the next Act, to Femi Osofisan, for his very useful comments, and to Tanure Ojaide, for all his support and encouragement!

Abdul-Rasheed Na'Allah
July 2018

Pioneer Cast

This play, now revised, was first performed by the Department of Performing Arts, Kwara State University, in celebration of 11/11, the anniversary of the assumption of Office of the Emir of Ilorin, His Royal Highness, Alhaji Ibrahim Sulu Gambari, to the throne of his ancestors, on 11 November 2015, at the Kwara State Council of Arts and Culture Complex, Ilorin, at 7pm.

Original Crew
Executive Producer: *Abdul-Rasheed Na'Allah*
Producer/Artistic Director: *Yemi Atanda*
Stage Manager: *Lanre Agboola*
Tech. Director/Set Designer: *Tosho Awogbemi*
Costumer: *Abiola Fasoranti*
Make-up Artist: *Tayo Adenuga*
Business Manager: *Temitope Adedokun-Richard*
Props Manager: *Michael Fernandez*
Photographer: *Edwin Aiyudu*
Set Designer: *Tosho Awogbami*
Technical Assistant: *Gbenga Adumati & Jamiu Rafiu*

Cast
Mariama: *Alade Ololade*
Sakariyawu: *Aigoro O. Haleem*

Silifatu: *Babayeju Omolola*
Rafatu: *Jimoh Dolapo* Fatayi: *Olalekan Ajikobi*
Musibawu: *Ibironke Shalom*
Salami: *Olasunkanmi Omoboriowo*
Lamidi (Chairman): *Itidi Henry/Ezekiel Abayomi*
Alfa Layisi: *Olayiwola Mohammed*
Mufutawu: *Oladipupo Adeleke Ishaq*

Councillors
Shogbesan Olalekan
Dankazeem Abdulkhalid
Owolbi David
Adebisi owoyele

Other Students
Busari Sukura
Jatto Adesewa
Barakat TemitopeAlao
Adeola Malik
Mama Baraka Family: *Aisha Elelu*
Alhaja Hawawu: *Bisola Mohammed*
Alhaji Batimoluwasi: *Victor Adeleke*
Poor Woman: *Aisha Umar*
Chairman's Wife: *Rasheedat Aliu*
Mama Mufutawu: *Balikis Adisa*
Mama Fatayi's friend: *Latifat Ayanponle*
Mama Fatayi's Family: *Nimota Alao*

Market People
Grace Olaitan Oladimeji
Omogaraeni Babalola

Deborah Afolayan

Shijuade Adegbemile

Aiyeola Anuoluwapo

Gertrude Khama

Adenike Adeyemi

 Temitope Aromukeye

Mary Jadesola Ajayi

Timileyin Adedoyin

David Adelakun (Alhaji Dangote)

Ibrahim Azeez

Wuraola Badmus

Omolola Oladokun

Oyebanke Komolafe

Victor Adeleke

Stage Hands
Elizabeth Funke Odejide

Stanley Michael

Titilayo Muyiwa

Moshood Abiola Shittu

Grace Olaitan Oladimeji

Aminat Oluwalogbon

Ajide Azeez

Sijuade Adegbemile

Zainab Oshagbemi

Marcy Brownson

Orchestra
Funmilola Owolabi

Bukola Yusuph

Uduak Cletus
Sunmbo Olatunji
Abiodun Araoye
Gbohunmi Durojaye
Itunu Adewuyi
Damilola Owolabi
Latifat Olaide

Drummers
Victor Adeleke
Tolulope Ogunrinde
Isaac Olaniyan
Shogbesan Olalekan
David Owolabi
Timileyin Adedoyin

Characters

Mariama: a true community woman, not-yet married, a secondary school teacher

Sakariyawu: Mariama's father, called Baba by his children

Silifatu: Mariama's mother, called Mama by her children; also called Mama Fatayi by some, perhaps the most respected blind person in the community

Rafatu: Mariama's childhood friend, radical, no-nonsense

Fatayi: Mariama's younger brother,

Councillor I

Counsellor II

Lamidi: Ile-Eni Local Government Chairman, pot-bellied, with unusual moustache

Aafa Layisi: a Quranic teacher, always with a slight turban

Mufutawu: a Quranic school student, as thin as a person could be

Student I

Student II

Other students

Jamaa: parents and others

Voice

Voices

Wolima Party: A party of Quranic School students, parents, and others walking the street accompanying the Wolima students

Prelude

A modern African city at first sight! Urban, with a mixture of rural and urban modernity. African and Islamic cultural and artistic symbols and images abound. Also abound, a few British-style housing structures, e.g., courthouses, prisons, banks, classrooms, offices, and old government official houses with boys' quarters all at the city's outskirts. Mainly traditional Yoruba and Hausa house structures with corrugated iron sheets in downtown areas. Calls to Muslim prayers are heard five times daily from all directions, far and near, and soon sounds of Quranic recitations come through from ongoing *salats*, Muslim ritual prayers. And as they subside, words, sentences, discussions, even laughter come from all directors, mainly in Yoruba, but also in Hausa, Nupe and English. The city is a multilingual city of Yoruba, Hausa, Fulani, Nupe, Baruba and Kemberi ancestries. The city's name is *Ile-Eni*, a Yoruba phrase for "people's house". African oral performance scenes, poetry, narratives, spring up randomly around the city.

12

Act 1

[6pm on Thursday, the day already begins to darken in Ile-Eni. It is Harmattan season. The air is dry and cold. As a sign of the Harmattan cold, Mariama wears her sweaters and occasionally still shivers from the intense cold. She's sitting on a bench, sometimes walks around in the corridor of her nuclear family's section of the large extended family compound]

Mariama: [sitting alone on a bench, her scarf tied around her head, her hands holding her head, tears in her eyes; her crying can be heard as her voice sometimes grows shaky] Eh, eh, eh-eh-eh! Oh Allah!

Why must it come to this, eh! Eh-eh-eh-eh!

[Opens her palms, raises her hands and looks up]

Oh my God, you do not abandon your servant. This is the time the Chameleon must not be stopped from assuming the colour it likes to brandish as its own. Or are you tired of me, oh Allah? The world will say she's finished.

Oh yes, she's finished! She's now an *adelebo*-- clearly a grown up woman, twenty years old, has refused to marry. We've not seen any man with her.

She's a successful teacher, or so we hear, but what is she doing teaching other people's children when she's not married to bring her own to the world!

They will say perhaps she has a curse on her head. Oh yes, a curse.

They will say, "She's beautiful, truly represents a well brought-up lady. Why has she failed to get married? She will be a terrible role model in the community!" Oh, I am already one, am I not, Allah?

[Hands down, both hands simultaneously beat her thighs, then each other and back on her thighs] When the cow feels the sharp pain of the knife cutting through its throat, it yells. But what else can it do? Its legs have been held down, its eyes have been closed, and the butchers are excited by their expectation to eat the meat, forgetting to think of the pain the cow goes through.

[suddenly breaking into song, her voice carrying the burden of her worries]

> Oju ni Malu nro, obe o dara l'orun o
> Oju ni Malu nro, obe o dara l'orun o
> Obe o dara lorun o, obe o dara l'orun o
> Oju ni Malu nro, obe o dara l'orun o![1]

Sakariyawu: [coming from outside, wearing a big green agbada gown and a nicely designed multi-coloured cap to match, speaks sarcastically, trying, as usual to be jovial]: My daughter, the cow better bears the pain, because the butcher in Ipata Market Will feed his family.

He needs the cow's meat to sell and make money for his children.

Or can you tell Fatayi that he will not have meat with his tuwo tonight, because we like to pity cow for the pain it goes through?

---

[1] Meaning, "The cow only bears the pain; knife isn't a good visitor to the throat"

My daughter, the cow will have to bear the pain. We have no other way of ensuring that our *amala*'s toes knock no corner on its way to our stomachs.

It is the meat that makes *amala*'s journey smooth [laughing, he approaches his daughter on the bench] ha-ha-ha!

Mariama: [initially taken aback by the sudden appearance of her father during her singing, kneels]
You're welcome my father, I hope the day is sweet.

Sakariyau *[looking at her on the ground]* Don't you hear when our people say, "it is a person's wish to prolong the eating of meat in his mouth, but the pull of the throat would not permit?"
[his right hand on her head]
Thank you my daughter. Today is indeed sweet-- it is sweeter, and I hope everything is good with you, too. I hear some sadness in your voice. Your face looks dull... is anything the matter?

Mariama: *[gets up, collects the small nylon bag in her father's left hand]* Let me help you with this. No, nothing is wrong-- just a little reflection on my life and our society. You know the daughter you gave birth to. The hen's feathers are spread to house its little children, my hen's eyes would shed tears if its children die from lack of warmth!

Sakariyawu: *[first walking towards his room, his daughter follows, both then suddenly stop, facing each other]*

Elaloro! My daughter, what are the lizards and toads in your words?

When a child cuts a tree from the bottom it is the elder who knows where the tree will fall. Your words express an in-depth thought, my daughter.

But, I'm still at a loss.

The hen should be celebrating for having feathers and for her tenderness for her children. She should be happy that it is she that can lay eggs and has feathers to keep the children warm. What can the cock do, other than to crow and peck on the hen?

Elaloro, let's break your utterance into pieces, my daughter! The words I hear from your mouth do not match the voice that utters them. Your voice seems shaky from sorrow, yet your words are those of pride, the mother's pride that she alone can make!

Mariama: I am not sad, father. My cries are cries of reflection. I have worked so hard, attained my teacher's certification at the University level that is the envy of my peers... external inspectors have judged me among the best teachers in my school and at their recent visit. They presented me as a role model. My peers clapped and hailed me as the Queen Teacher of Iwanu Nasiru-Deen Secondary School...

Sakariyawu: *[cuts in]* What about your Headteacher? Is he the problem? He still gives you problems, doesn't he? Tell me, is he sad that you, my daughter, have impressed the inspectors and impressed your peers? The hen's feathers do not fall for no reason. Why can't he be happy for my hardworking daughter? He is the aged cock who doesn't know itself as an elder! Don't worry, my daughter, we'll report him to Allah.

Our people have rightly said that it is Allah who measures out a right *seriya* for a wicked person. You're the cow without a tail, and God Almighty will chase away the flies for you!

Mariama: [*with a puzzling look at her father*] Oh my father, did I tell you my Principal was the problem? When was the last time I reported him to you?

Sakariyawu: [*not listening*] I shall have to tell our Magaji, and a party shall be sent to his extended family so that his family can plead with him to leave my daughter alone. Your mother and I have never wished anything bad for anyone's child, why would anybody wish evil for ours? Or, do ...

Mariama: [*interrupting her father, speaking at a louder voice*] My Baba! My Baba! How many times have I called you?

Sakariyawu: My daughter, you have called me two times. What?

Mariama: You're not listening to me. My Principal is not the problem I am worrying about, at least not at this time. Besides, what more *seriya* do you want Allah to measure out to him beside what God has already sentenced him to for his many sins?

His wickedness has never subsided. Even yesterday, he destroyed an innocent teacher's record, claiming to the inspectors that the young man refused to participate in any school activities when it was he who hated the sight of the young man and would not assign him to any school duty.

God's *seriya*, yet, is the severest.

The Principal has no child of his own. He has taken his third wife, and after two years, even that wife hasn't borne him a child. The rumour is that he has no patience with his wives.

Yes, our people's adage can never be faulted. God is the Almighty that measures out appropriate seriya to the deafest human being who won't hear His admonitions and wouldn't listen to His words.

And sometimes Allah does what is good and human beings think He's done a bad thing.

Who knows, the head-teacher might have even hated his own children if Allah had given him some and perhaps he might have starved them to death!

He's become a laughing stock in the community and people say he is a sheep who calls himself a he-goat!

[talking more slowly, as if giving each word its full weight]

But my Baba, I swear to you that the Principal is not my problem this time. I was only reflecting on my own life. At twenty-four years of age, though a successful teacher, my ripe feathers have not attracted a suitor. I have not seen the right man to take me to the most honourable house of motherhood.

You gave me birth; I want to give birth to children of my own! You have taught me, that marriage is the tradition of our prophet!

Sakariyawu: [*sobers, becomes emotional*] Settle down, my daughter, let me pray for you. [*putting his right hand on her head*]

Mariama: [*kneeling*] Thank you my father, I know your prayers and those of my mother have never ceased to keep me company.
You have both encouraged me to make my own choice of a husband and Allah willing, my moon will attract its admirer and we shall soon fetch my own cola nut.

Sakariyawu: [*clears his voice*] Yes, my daughter, your cola nut shall be distributed to near and far, inside and outside of Ile-Eni. You will be as happy as the moon whose teeth are sharp enough that they lighten the world.

Mariama: *Aamin, aamin.*

Sakariyawu: Your world will be as rich as the sky and as brilliant as the sun.
The sky, with cloud or without cloud, rains on the earth and presents shining stars in the night. Like the sky, you'll rain-- rain any time of the day and it would not be limited to a season, because even some Harmattan seasons give us rain, however limited.

Mariama: *Aamin, kunfayakun,* my Baba, *aamin!*

Sakariyawu: With each new day that emerges, you'll emerge
like that new day.
Every year, my daughter, you'll count your blessings
and celebrate new heights.

Mariama: [tears showing on her face, seems totally moved]
Aamin, kunfayakun, my Baba, you'll live long.
You and Mama will reap the fruits of your labour.

Sakariyawu: You may stand up now and don't you cry again.
So many people approached me and also approached
the family asking to marry you for their sons. My
childhood friend even wanted you for a wife.
We have turned all this down as you know.
Your mother and I will wait for you to get your own
choice. That is how we want it. This time next year, it
shall be your turn and we shall gather your cola nut.
Fatayi your brother is still young and making steady
progress in school. Tomorrow he will also have a small
Quran graduation. We're due for Allah's blessings, not
His *seriya*.
My daughter, from this week we'll begin to count and
Allah will make it your turn. Get your fingers ready.
With Allah's support, we'll soon count your *alamisi* for
your wedding!
[*Turns back and walks toward his room*]
My child, bring my bag inside and go about your
evening. I'm already late for *maghrib* prayers. Is your
mother not at home yet? Where is Fatayi? Tell Fatayi to
see me.

Mariama: *[follows her father]* My gratitude will never cease, Baba. Mama has gone to buy *irú* from the market. She plans to make your delicious soup. I will make the fire for dinner after my *salat*. Mother and Fatayi would join soon. *[Enters her father's room]*

Act 2

[8:15pm, in Sakariyawu's room. He is sitting on a sofa dozing off. An electric florescent can be seen close to the ceiling fan, but the only light in the room is from the kerosene lamp on a table close to the window. There are two sofas in the room; Sakariyawu is sitting in the one closer to the table by the window. The other sofa is at the far end of the room directly facing the window. In a corner far removed is Sakariyawu's salat carpet, a beautiful salat carpet with a magnificent mosque diagram. The carpet is spread out and rosary and a prayer book are right on it. One can see several signs that the carpet has recently been used. Close to it are also a cup and a plate with a small remnant of rice and a spoon inside]

Silifatu: *[enters, no knock is heard, the sound of her walking stick gives notice of her arrival]* Baba Fatayi, Baba Fatayi!

Sakariyawu: *[startles out of sleep]* Eh, eh! Who's that? *[first, sees the stick]* Oh, Mama Fatayi, it's you!

Silifatu: It is me. *[facing the direction of Sakariyawu's voice, hearing the noises from the plates Sakariyawu kicked as he startled]*. I didn't realize your dinner plates were still lying here. Fatayi should have come to collect them.

Sakariyawu: Oh, I dozed off. I still have some prayers to do for my daughter. Your *amala* was the straight way to my heaven! The *irú* ensured it was direct to paradise! Your mother did well to train you to be such a great cook.

Silifatu: [*smiling to herself, pretending as if she had not heard Sakariyawu's comments; sitting down as she feels with her hand the right place to sit*] Have you informed your brothers about Fatayi's *wolima*? We must arrive early enough tomorrow morning, and then we'll return to the Quranic school with the *wolima* party after the Friday prayers tomorrow.

Sakariyawu: My wife, this is only his ending of the fortieth chapter of the Quran. He still has twenty more chapters to go. A person gets his or her water pot filled up before lifting it to the head to go home. What is the use of mobilizing the entire family when we still need more water to fill his pot? Let children from our extended family go to support their brother. You and your sister could also be there. I will give you fifty naira for the *wolima* money. I am proud of our son. At 13, he's done me proud and I'm sure he'll complete the Quran by next year or at 15.
Oh Allah, accept my prayers for Fatayi and his sister. Let them remain shining stars in our community.

Silifatu: Aamin, my husband. They are core children. They are children enough for everyone to ask Allah for children of their kind. We will need more than fifty naira. Your pocket will not dry, my husband [*'looking' up in prayers*].

More will replace your expenses in the name of Mohammed. I have made enough food; we'll all have more than enough to eat and to distribute to well-wishers. My own parents and their entire compound will be there. This is our only son [*breaking into a light songs and a light dance*]:

> *Omo mi alabi, tori re mo nse nsise*
> *Eh-eh o*
> *Omo ni o jogun mi amin o!*
>
> *Omo mi alabi, tori re mo nse nsise*
> *Eh-eh o*
> *Omo ni o jogun mi amin o!*[2]

[hears a knock on the door and stops dancing and singing]

Lamidi: [in big gown and a cap to match; knocks on the door] *Gafara, gafara o! Sakariyawu*, are you in?

Silifatu: [*recognizes the voice, then to her husband*] You have a guest, Lamidi, Sule's father. I'll get him some water. [*Greets the guest through movement only, no exchange of words, then departs*]

Sakariyawu: Oh, the Chairman! [*gets up, walks to the door to receive his guest*] To God belongs *gafara*. We do not see your masquerade outside of his den [*beckoning him*

---

[2] "My son Alabi, I work for you
Eh-eh o
I shall be leaving a child to inherit me (when I die), oh amen!"

24

inside with a gesticulation with his hand]. For what have we earned the visit of the lion of the forest?

Lamidi: [*smiling, shaking Sakariyawu's hand as he touches his own pot belly with his other hand, then gesticulating with both hands*] My brother, you know, I will always come to see you. What is *okuku* doing that it will not come towards the weaver? What is the nail doing that it would refuse to keep the finger company? What is the tongue doing that it will not pay a visit to the teeth? What is a human voice without his or her throat? Who am I without the good will of my lords and benefactors?

Sakariyawu: [*ushering him to a sofa*] Eh-eh, Chairman, the Chairman! I am not surprised. Today's politicians' mouths are like the white man's salt.

Lamidi: [smiling profusely as he beats his own stomach]: No, it is not a sugar mouth. It is the true mouth of your brother, the original local mouth of your brother! We're brothers; we grew together right here in Ile-Eni!

Sakariyawu: Come on, Chairman! I don't know we're still brothers. It is true we grew up together, but you're a big man now. [*looks him from head to toe and back to his protruding pot belly*] Look at your cloth, the material is imported from London, not our local *Ile-Eni* weave or the type you wore before with us—the type bought from Jankara Market in Lagos. Your shoes are like the ones my daughter told me were called Italian Shine. She said it's the favourite of you men politicians [*almost touching his face*].

Your skin itself is changing colour or have you also imported skin lately? I also heard that you and your family have moved to your new duplex in the Government Reservation Area [*gazes at the stomach*]. You have also become pregnant, the rich man's pregnancy.

[*Lamidi smiles profusely as he beats again on his own stomach*].

Now, I know election is next month and I do appreciate seeing you, but it was almost four years ago that you came to our area, let alone enter my own house. Oh, yes, I remember, it was a time like this, the election was one month away and you asked us to vote for a change. Are you here asking us to vote for another change, my brother?! I think it's now that we deserve a change!

Lamidi: [seems to be overwhelmed, suddenly sweating] Oh, my brother, thank you so much. It's been so tight at the office you put us in. It was not the desire of the masquerade not to come to visit the people he leaves behind even if they are in the market. The noise of selling and buying are only sweet to his ears. But indeed my brother, it is the water in the soup pot that is too much rather than the soup ingredients. [looks toward the door]

Silifatu: [*entering, with a cup on one hand and her stick on the other*] Here, Baba Alufa, this is water for you to drink. What food can I get you?

26

Lamidi: [*sighs, collecting the cup of water, helping to lead Silifat to her seat*]. My wife, thank you so much. It is already late and I am sorry to disturb your peace [drinks from the cup, stops to talk, facing Sakariyawu].

Actually, the reason I came was that I heard your son Fatayi would be celebrating *wolimat* tomorrow. Some of my councillors and I would like to celebrate with you. We know how important this is to you two [*facing Silifatu*]. He is your one and only son and we would like to be there for you. After all, what are we doing in the office that is more than sharing in the good and its other side with our people?

Silifatu: [mood brightens up] Oh, may Allah assist in the performance of your work! This will indeed bring honour to my family. We have to be there early, before the sun gets to the middle of the sky. Then we shall follow the *wolima* children back to the Quranic school after Friday prayers.

Lamidi: We'll be there at both times. [*Empties the cup and hands it back to Silifatu, rubbing his stomach*] We'll be there.

Silifat: [on her feet] Oh, thank you, we'll see you tomorrow then [stepping out]

Sakariyawu: How did you hear about Fatayi's *wolima*? It is just the end of his fortieth chapters—it's no big deal.

Lamidi: [*laughs and beats his stomach*] There's nothing happening in the community without my knowledge. You appointed me Local Government Council Chairman, remember? Our people's activities are my first interest.

Sakariyawu: Indeed. But, you don't have to worry. I myself will not be there. It is not important to leave your tight schedule for a fortieth chapter proficiency celebration *Wolima*.

Lamidi: Oh, tell that to Mama Fatayi. This is among the greatest achievements for you two. I, together with my right-hand councillors, would like to come and celebrate with your son and your family.

Sakariyawu: So, the election-- are we voting for a change?

Lamidi: Oh, about that... you know you're highly respected in all the surrounding areas, and you're among the favorites of mine, your family is really a great family...

Sakariyawu: Chairman, are we voting for a change?

Lamidi: Oh, what we really need now is stability. I know it was not easy in the last four years. All our plans are meeting implementation difficulty. The budget has not been that great and the problem is directly from the Federal Government ...

Sakariyawu: So we need a change.

Lamidi: [gesticulating rather heavily] What I am trying to say is that we do not need a change in leadership, so that we can ensure the plans we already announced will be immediately implemented once we are re-elected. I need your support, Sakariyawu. You know our friendship dates back to our childhood. Our parents were family friends, my great grand family married from your great grand family. We're actually a family. I would like you to join me, campaign to the people for me.

Sakariyawu: Is that what your attendance at Fatayi's *wolima* is about? Is that what—

Lamidi: *[getting up from sofa, holding his belly as if it might fall down]* I must be going now. It's already well past 10pm. I am so sorry for taking your time when you should be sleeping. I knew it was the best time to meet you. *[Stepping out]*

Sakariyawu: *[seeing him out]* The mouse knows when the cat plays its hide and seek. It is not for nothing that it has the fastest feet!

Lamidi: [pretends he doesn't hear, giving Sakariyawu his hand] Thank you very much. Sleep well. We will see you at *wolimat* tomorrow.

Sakariyawu: *[stops at the door]* We will all sleep well. Greet your household.

29

Lamidi: [departs] Bye, bye.

Sakariyawu: *[closing his door]* Bye, bye *[as he puts off the light, his voice can be heard]* Oh, God's *seriya*, where are you!

Lights out!

Act 3

[10am Friday morning. The day is growing rather hot from the eagerly burning sun, although the Harmattan cold can still be felt in the air. Al-Nur Quranic School is filling up with wolima students and their parents and well-wishers as well as some other students from the school. It is the Iya-Adini family compound and the Quranic School is a building at the center of the compound. It is large and spacious with mats, benches, and chairs arranged neatly in lines and groups in readiness for the wolima event. Guests and students are already taking their seats. Wala, reading wooden slates, and tira, Islamic religious books, including several smaller Quranic books, can be seen by the corner in traditional shelves and tables. Wolima students can be recognized as dressed in blue jalabiya with caps to match. Aafa Layisi, the Quranic School teacher, is dressed in a big blue gown with a blue cap. He holds a microphone and speaks directly to it. Most women wear traditional iro and buba, and rising head ties covered with long scarves that fall on their shoulders. It is now getting noisy]

Aafa Layisi: [standing, a complete view of all participants]:
　　　Aasitu! Aassituu lillahi!

Jamaa: [*single murmur, then total silence, everyone looking at Aafa*] *Aasituu!*

Aafa Layisi: [*clears his voice, then continues*] Please be silent in the name of God! If an assignment would not delay a person, a person should not delay the assignment. Our assignment today is a pleasurable and joyous one, the *wolima* we're about to start! Please if you haven't got a seat, find yourself one that is comfortable for you. If you drive a car on my stomach today, it will run very smoothly over it.

Jamaa: [*some from them*] Ha-ha-ha

Aafa Layisi: The best of the human beings is he who is grateful to Allah for Allah's bounties to us. I, Aafa Layisi, here say to you God that I am grateful.

Jamaa: [*each mentioning his or her name*] I, here say to you God that I am grateful!

Aafa Layisi: I am grateful

Jamaa: I am grateful!

Aafa Layisi: Indeed. Whoever knows how to think would know how to show gratitude. I join all you parents in saying, *alhamdulillahi*! [*Sees Ile-Eni Local Government Chairman with two LG councilors coming in*] Here, we're having important guests! [to the gathering] All you *jamaa* [*recite with me*]:
Subhanallah alhamdulillah laailaha ilallah

Jamaa: [singing] *Subhanallah alhamdulillah, laailaha ilallah*
Subhanallah alhamdulillah, laailaha ilallah

Subhanallah alhamdulillah, laailaha ilallah

Aaafa Layisi: [*beckons on the important guests to the front row*]
Please here! [*sings with the Jamaa*] Suhanallah!

Jamaa: *...alhamdulillah, lailaha ilallah*
Subhanallah alhamdulillah, lailaha ilallah
Subhanallah alhamdulillah, lailaha ilallah

[*Suddenly, Aafa Layisi seems overwhelmed with
excitement, changes song*]

Maraba o, maraba,
Alhaji, maraba, Alhaja, maraba[3]
Chairman, *maraba*
Maraba o, maraba
Counsellor *maraba, Alhaja, maraba*!

[*He walks to a chair close to Lamidi, shakes hands with
Lamidi and sits*]

Aafa Layisi: [*returns to position*] Salu alanabiyyi kareem!

Jamaa: [in unison] *Salallahu Alayhi wassalam!*

Aafa Layisi: [waving his right hand to stop singing, facing the
Local Government Chairman and Counsellors] The
leading masquerade leaves his cult house last. He

---

[3] "Welcome o, welcome
Alhaji, welcome, Alhaja, welcome"

arrives last at his destination. We have them here, our
gbajumo! Today, politicians meet business tycoons.
Today, we will know the other names money is called.
[*Looking at his students*]
Are we ready?

Students: Yes!

Aafa Layisi: We must start with prayers. It is a person's
prayers that succeed with God, not a person's strength
[*looking at the gathering, targeting the parents*]. One of
your children will pray for us. *Allahu Akbar*! Your
children are now Islamic scholars. Stop seeing them as
children: he who knows how to read the Quran is not a
child! [*Pointing at one student, about 10 years old*]
Mufutawu, pray for us! [*looks at Mufutawu's parents,
smiles, seems happy with himself*]

Mufutawu: [*comes out, takes the microphone closer to his
mouth, spreading his right hand palm also nearer his
mouth, uses traditional Ile-Eni recitation voice, reads
from the Quran off his head*] Authu billahi mina shaytani
Rajeemi, bismillahi Raheemi Raheemi.
*Wa qaluu Alhamdulillahi lathii sodaqhnaa wa'adahu wa-
aorathnaa'l-ardha natabawwau minal jannati haethu
nasha'u fani'ima 'ajrul'aamiliina. Wataraa'lmalaaikata
haafiina min haolil 'arshi yusabbihuuna
bihamdirabbihim waqhadhiya baenahum bilhaqqhi wa
qhiilalhamdulillahi rabbilhaalamiina.*

34

Jamaa: [*some visibly moved, Mufutawu's mom is seen with tears, gets up pointing a naira note at her Mufutawu*] Allaaaaaahu Akbar!

Aafa Layisi: [*with pride*] This is what your children have become, Islamic scholars! It is the egg that becomes the rooster [looking from one side to the other, targeting parents]. Parents! Your roosters are not edible by any human being that is born of woman. Not even those born by the glass houses of the white man! Oh, yes, it is, white man, the *yaudi*, for long born children out of cylinders.

Jamaa: *Allahu Akbar!*

Counsellor I: [*stands*] Mufutawu, have this, God will increase your *alubarika*! [*hands him a single 100 naira note, but does not mention the amount. More parents and well-wishers, mainly elderly, give coins or naira notes in much smaller denominations*]

Lamidi: [stands, one hand in his pocket, the other on his belly] Aafa, we're proud of your achievements...[*looks back, sideways and front*] Parents, aren't we? [*No one seems to respond*]
Where is the child who prayed now, Mufutawu, have this [*brings sets of naira notes from his pocket*] Here is 1000 naira! [*hands it to Mufutawu. Looks front, back and sideways, slowly sits down, a few parents are seen speaking silently to each other, some eyeing Lamidi with disapproval*]

Aafa Layisi: Oh, we have just allowed you a taste from the soup, we haven't started to eat yet. Chairman the Chairman. *Allahu Akbar!*

Jamaa: *Allahu Akbar!*

Aafa Layisi: [*takes money from Mufutawu, speaks to his ears, and together, they start, singing*] *Eyin tee kewu ekuya!*

Other Students: *Awa n jaye kalamu, Ina-l hakku nasiira, wa akali adada*!

> *Eyin teekewu eku iya,*
> *Awa n jaye kalamu*
> *Ina-l hakku nasira*
> *Wa akali adada!*[4]

> *Eyin teekewu eku iya,*
> *Awa n jaye kalamu*
> *Ina-l hakku nasira*
> *Wa akali adada!*

Aafa Layisi: [*waves to students to stop*] Praise God!

Jamaa: *Allahu Akbar!*

---

[4] You who won't learn the Quran, you're suffering indeed!
We're enjoying our world from the blessings of the pen
The truth is clear to us
And yes, we're enjoying indeed!

Aafa Layisi: It's now time [*turn to his students*] Wolima students, come out! [*pointing at his right side*] all stand here. Only two sets of students are graduating today, 2 have completed 40 chapters, 3, completed the entire Quran and will start the *Fik-hu* in the next stage. 5 of them altogether. Praise Allah!

Jamaa: *Allahu Akbar!*

Aafa Layisi: We'll start from those who have completed 40 chapters, then move to those that have finished the entire Quran. It is the biggest masquerade that dances last! [*some parents are seen nodding their heads in agreement*]
But you have to buy them *alubarika*-- it is by your spending today that you will show your love for them, because they have made you proud and you want God to bless them [*a voice is heard from the gathering*]

Voice: These Aafas with love for money! [*some parents seen nodding their heads in agreement, some smile*]

Aafa Layisi: [continues, ignoring the comment] You buy your children *alubarika*, this is the day, parents! When each child is called to the stage to read, we'll see those who love their children most, the people who want the greatest *alubarika* for their children. God's blessings have to be earned! Now [*turning to wolima students*] Fatayi, [*handing him the microphone*] Fatayi!

[Fatayi's mom almost jumps from happiness, ignoring her walking stick and being helped by a person, showering her son with money, all naira notes; likewise with her parents and others who come with her to the wolima-- some put money in the box, some on Fatayi's forehead, some on his hand, and some just throw money at him. A student is seen taking the money and putting all inside the box. Lamidi first waits and then moves forward, collects the microphone from Mufutawu]

Lamidi: [clears his throat, as he beats his belly with pride] Kha-kha! Aafa, we join you in expressing gratitude to God. [stops talking for effect, then turning to the gathering, continues] Today is a great day in Ile-Eni, our children continue to complete the Quran and become Islamic scholars. I join the parents to thank God. If one's masquerade knows how to dance well, one's head swells! My head swells today, not only for Fatayi and his parents whom I followed here today, but for all parents and students here.

As Chairman of Ile-Eni Local Government Council, I am here for all of you. [pointing at the councillors] And these councillors are here for you too. We are a team, even within our National Party. We formed a special team! *[noise is beginning to build. Some from the audience seem to be protesting Lamidi's statements, but he continues]* [rubs his belly] I would like to assure you that we love our Islam and we love the people. This is not about the next election.

Voice: *[from the gathering]* Of course it is!

Voices: Sit down! We're here for the students.

[*Aafa Layisi now seems a little anxious but still smiling. Mama Fatayi can be seen really furious at Lamidi, the anger can be seen in the way she faces Lamidi and other councillors from her seat, now holding her sticks as if to lash someone*]

Lamidi: [*ignoring the protests*] Indeed election is very close, just next month. Well, this is about you our people. It is about our love for you!

Mama Fatayi: [*spontaneous, the anger shows with ferocity*] Love for money! For money!

Lamidi: [*stops, seems shocked at Mama Fatayi's sudden burst*] I am sorry. [*Continues, sees Aafa has stopped smiling and looking a bit disturbed*]. We're ready to spend money here today for these students' *alubarika*. I have asked my councillors to arrange for food and soft drinks and some will be brought to the Friday Prayers today. We will be back here after Jumaa salat[5] and as for what we will spend here, you haven't seen anything yet. The land will open marvelling at our love for you people of Ile Eni. What better way to show our love than asking *alubarika* for your children?

Aafa Layisi: [*smiling*] *alubarika* for Fatayi, *alubarika*...

---

[5] Friday Prayers or Jumaa or Jumaa salat refers to one and the same thing

Parent: [stands, very furious, but makes her statement very slowly, all fall silent, Aafa seems to begin to shake from anxiety] I do not blame Aafa for asking for *alubarika, alubarika*, no one pays them salary, yet they teach our children and depend only on Thursday alms, which most parents don't pay.

[*Looks round at parents*]

It is from one's work that one eats, so our people say!

[*Looks at Lamidi and councillors with despise*]

And our politicians, [*changing her voice to imitate Lamidi's, rubbing her stomach*] "Oh, we love our people, we love our people." They build personal mansions the fortnight after they get elected and claim they love the people. Our children have become *almajiri* on the street, and their teachers have become *alubara*.[6]

No, they can neglect the Quranic schools, refuse to recognize their teachers. They can neglect our values and turn our children to hooligans roaming the streets.

[*Looking at Lamidi and his councillors*]

Shame. [*Walks over to put money in the box, touches Fatayi's head and returns to her seat*]

Lamidi and councillors: [to Parent] Our mother!

Lamidi: Our mother is angry at us [*brings out money, looks at Fatayi*]. Fatayi, good child. This is two thousand. And this is only a beginning.

---

[6] Both *almajiri* and *alubara* are beggars as used in this context, however *almajiri* are also used for Quranic school pupils seeking food, assistance or sponsorship, while *alubara* is clearly a person driven to beg because of poverty or deformity, even simply because of being poor or no salary despite working hard.

[*Aafa Laisi is seen now to resume smiling, though not as broadly as before*]

Aafa, pray for *alubarika*. Today is the today. Today is the day of a person sent on an errand! We have an errand for our people in Aafa Laisi's School today. We'll let you continue the *wolima*.

[*looks at the front, in the back, and sideways*]

Parents, please convey our message of love to all our people. We're going for another appointment but will see you all after *juma'a salat*. We'll be there for Ile-Eni's children!

Aafa Layisi: Now [*to Fatayi*] Come closer and start to read...

[*Suddenly remembers that Lamidi and councillors are about to leave, waves at his students and collects the microphone*]

Chairman the Chairman!

[*starts to sing, students chorus the refrain, as Lamidi and councillors walk out*]

Aafa: *Ebawa ki* Lamidi *po dabo,*

Students: *Ma'asalama odabo o*

Aafa: *Eki awon gbajumo po dabo*

Students: Ma'asalama odabo o

Aafa: *Eki Lamidi po dabo*

Students: *Ma'asalama odabo o!*

41

[*Aafa Layisi resumes the wolima rites, starting with Fatayi; returns the microphone to Fatayi, suddenly seen thinking hard, quickly looking every side, that is what he does whenever he sees or talks to Fatayi, since the day Fatayi's sister, Mariama, accompanied Fatayi to the Quranic School, and he set his eyes on Mariama for the first time.*]

Fatayi: [*using the traditional Ile-Eni voice*] Authu billahi mina Shaytani Rajeemi, Bismillani Rahmani Raheem, Wa...

Act 4

[2:30 Friday afternoon, the Sun is fast moving from the middle of the sky in its journey towards the West. It is scorching; Harmattan cold is completely overpowered at this time of the day. Jumaa salat has just finished and faithfuls of all ages and genders are seen returning home, carrying prayer mats and mostly counting rosaries as they walk. Some Al-Nur Quranic School students and their Wolima celebrants in white turbans on blue jalabiya are walking the streets as part of the last leg of their Wolima celebration. They are seen singing as they walk. The party is approaching the school intensifying their songs and performances. Everyone is sweating and few are seen fanning their bodies while walking in excitement. Parents of the Wolima students, Lamidi, and the councilors are seen walking with the Wolima students. Three of the students carry crates of soft drinks, boxes of biscuits, and other kinds of crackers, distributing to those who like to eat. Fatayi's mother with her walking stick, Silifatu and Mariama, in white head covers, are walking together, a bit far behind, talking rather very actively as others in front sing and dance. Rafatu, in carefully packed jerry curled hair with flowers hanging in front, is singing and dancing with the group in front, seems now to be walking deliberately more slowly so that Mariama and her mom could catch up with her]

Rafatu: [singing and dancing simultaneously with the group, shaking her head to the rhythm]

Boba sepe aeku laye o
Aba ba Muhammadu
Aba ba Muammada
Oke Mefa le egbaaji
Awo o ba kan ma laye
Toreta fun Musa o
Injila fun Yisa
Sebura fun Dauda
Alkurani fun Onsela[7]

[*Now out of rhyme with the group, looking back, she seems to be calculating with her eyes that Mariama would soon catch up with her. She smiles and sings, making her shoulders go up and down to a new rhyme*]

Toreta fun Musa o
Injila fun Yisa o
Sebura fun Dauda o
Alkurani fun Onsenla

Toreta fun Musa o
Injila fun Yisa o
Sebura fun Dauda o
Alkurani fun Onsenla

---

[7] "If there wasn't death in this World/ We would have met Muhammadu alive/ We would have met Muhammada alive/ Thousands and thousands of them/ We didn't meet any in the World/ Toreta is for Moses/ Injila for Jesus/ Sebura for David/ Alkurani is for the lead messenger!"

Toreta fun Musa o
Injila fun Yisa o
Sebura fun Dauda o
Alkurani fun Onsenla

[Mariama catches up with Rafatu, sneaks in and out of her performance]

Rafatu & Mariama: *Toreta fun Musa o*
Injila fun Yisa o
Sabura fun Dauda o
Alkurani fun Onsenla

[Mariama stops, takes one look at Lamidi and his councilors, and as if something suddenly comes upon her, turns to her mom]

Mariama: Mama, I really don't like this a bit.

Silifatu: [*surprised*] What?

Mariama: He's using my brother's *wolima* to campaign for his re-election. Filth, stinking filth! Vultures consume only filth! This is not the place for him. I was ashamed how he stood up after the *salat* to announce my brother's *wolima* to the faithfuls.
[*Angry*]
In what ways is hawk related to guinea fowl, eh? How is bat connected to parrot? *Ehoro* and *Ejo* are not related!

Silifatu: He came pretending to be interested in us and in Fatayi's *wolima*.

He thinks we're the fowls for his food!

Rafatu: [*hearing, frowns*] Hún-ùn, what our leaders have now become, only God can rescue us from them. Yet, we must as a people tell them we're not horses to ride. He thinks Ile-Eni has forgotten his four years of atrocities in office. He thinks all the people are in slumber.
[*A bit silently, but with the most serious look she could muster, Silifatu and Mariama are looking and listening with rapt attention*]
To see him and his councillors like this walking with us all the way from *jumaa* mosque is a little wonder to me. It is fake humility to make our people think he could come down to their level or that he and his fellow vultures love God and His religion. When they want power they pretend to love the ordinary people, but their hatred for the common person starts to manifest publicly the moment they are elected. If we haven't punished them, ensuring *seriya* [*almost shouting*], *ka dawon ni seriya, ka dawon ni seriya*! If we haven't meted out *seriya* on them, they'll always ride us and put their loads on us like donkeys.

[*Aafa Layisi, suddenly appears, very apprehensive, listening to Mariama's words, as if never heard anything like them before*] It is as if they are eating our flesh [*almost bursting, reaches the peak of anger*]. People like Lamidi and many of his councillors should be sentenced to death-- or their hands cut off-- or something!

Silifatu: [*shocked, not believing what she hears*] What?!
[*pulling her daughter, as if suddenly remembers that they should be walking at par with the main wolima party. Rafatu follows.*]

Silifatu: [after what seems a recovery, now catches up with the main party, turns to Mariama and Rafatu and continues their discussion, Aafa Layisi following them closely, his eyes fixed on Mariama]

Aafa Layisi: [*as if wanting to pull Mariama from the back*] Those words you spoke, exactly as they are in the Quran. Teacher's wisdom is the wisdom of God! Every day in human beings' courts of law, it is the he-goat's thief, the person who stole bread, and the *Almajiri* who snatches other people's clothes to resell in order to get money to feed himself, they are the ones that are condemned to jail; in God's Court, those are saints! God Almighty condemns the pen robbers, the likes of our politicians, who take more than their own shares, to heavenly fare, from where there is no escape.

Rafatu: The way they look at the *aparo* bird, it is as if it should end up in their pots of soup. It is the bird's destiny that has kept it alive.
[*Notices it is just three or four meters away from the Quranic School. She looks at Aafa Layisi and sees glows in his eyes as he speaks and continues to look at Mariama with admiration. She pinches Mariama on her hand and says something into her ears. Both of them burst into*

*laughter, as the students break into songs. The wolima
students dance, their shoulders making the most active
movement. They are turning their heads left and right
and looking at each of their shoulders as they dance]*

> *Won buwaa won la susuka
> Annabi lafijo o
> Won buwaa won la susuka
> Annabi lafijo*[8]

*[Aafa Layisi's dancing steps are so joyously directed at
Mariama, that all students marvel at this newfound
dancing zeal of their teacher. Mariama and Rafatu
cannot stop laughing, Rafatu seems to derive a special
satisfaction dragging Mariama to Aafa Layisi and
whispering and clapping simultaneously towards her.
One of the students takes over as lead-singer. A Follow-
refrain performance by all others. Lamidi, joined by
councilors, also does a bit active dance, twisting their
buttocks, more as if dancing to a non-religious Bembe
music rather than a more subdued Ile-Eni Islamic
ceremony dance.]*

Student I: *Won buwaa won la susuka*

Wolima Party: *Annabi lafijo!*

---

[8] "They condemn us for wearing the turban
We only imitate our prophet
They condemn us for wearing the turban
We only imitate our prophet"

48

Student I:	*Won buwaa won la susuka*
Wolima Party:	*Annabi lafijo!*
Student I:	*Won buwaa won la susuka*
Wolima Party:	*Annabi lafijo!*
Student I:	*Won buwaa won la susuka*
Wolima Party:	*Annabi lafijo!*

[*more people are gathering-- attracted more by the Local Government chairman and councillors than by the wolima students. Silifatu stops dancing and chorusing, watching with an abstained look. Rafatu and Mariama move closer to Aafa Layisi, putting him in between them and dancing with him*]

Student I:	*Won buwaa won la susuka*
Wolima Party:	*Annabi lafijo!*
Student I:	*Won buwaa won la susuka*
Wolima Party:	*Annabi lafijo!*
Student I:	*Won buwaa won la susuka*
Wolima Party:	*Annabi lafijo!*
Student I:	*Won buwaa won la susuka*
Wolima Party:	*Annabi lafijo!*

49

[*One of the students comes forward, looking very involved with the performance. He smiles to himself and, hesitating a little bit, announces*]

Student II: *Asituu! Asituu! Asitu lillahi!* Please stop. [*Having difficulty stopping the songs and the dances, continues to appeal for silence*]

Rafatu: [*quickly pulls Mariama aside*] We have to talk. We have a lot to discuss when we get home today! The cloud of our day is heavy and rough and the precipitation may be pebbles and rock.

Mariama: *Elaloro*, Rafatu, *Elaloro*!

Rafatu: We'll talk more at home. Exercise some patience. It is our elders that say that a speech cannot be so difficult that will demand our fetching a knife to cut it. It is mouth that is needed to break it into pieces. We will break this into pieces at your house. The student is talking; let's hear him.

Student II: Asituu in the name of Allah!
[*everyone now stops, Lamidi seems to have the hardest time stopping himself*]
We're almost at the Quranic School.
It is time for the *wolima* students to withdraw to the school. They'll eat and rest a bit. Aafa Layisi will pray for them before they all depart to their homes. For our

parents, you will live to do more *wolima* for your children. [The Wolima Party choruses in unison]

Wolima Party: *Aamin!*

Student II: For the generous well-wishers, your river's sources will not dry up!

Wolima Party: *Aamin!*

Student II: Please go home and leave the *wolima* students. Now, it's time to go to the school [breaks into a farewell song with students and others chorusing as they walk away. Aafa Layisi doesn't seem in a hurry to leave Mariama and Rafatu, and Mariama seems a bit shy from this new behavior of the Quranic teacher, as Rafatu remains all smiles in mischief]:

> *Oniwolima ndupe funwa o!*

Chorus:	*Gbogbo wa na landupe folohun!*
Oniwolima ndupe funwa o!
Gbogbowa na landupe folohun![9]

---

[9] "Wolima students are expressing gratitude!
We all are expressing our gratitude to God!"

Act 5

[6:00 pm at Mariama's extended family compound. The Sun is still entering its shell and its light might be available for sitting outside. In front of Sakariawu's nuclear family section of the compound are Mariama and her friend Rafatu. We observe a vigorous debate that seems to be going on between the two friends]

Rafatu: You got me right; all of them should be sent to jail, and allowed to rot there. Finished. We'll have new leaders who aren't going to steal because they would learn from the lesson of their predecessors. They would know there are repercussions in taking the people for a ride.

Mariama: Now listen, this is what I'm trying to explain to you: how many teeth shall we count from a dilapidated mouth! Our parents call us ideologues because of radical solutions like yours, and I'm sure Mama would tell father that Mariama and his friend think the *seriya* for corrupt politicians is life imprisonment. Or even death as you said. No, I do not agree with you.

Rafatu: *[eyes showing/ filled with irritation]* I do not blame you. You're lucky, aren't you? Your father is a professional clothes weaver and got money to send you to school. There are millions of our people across this country, farmers, bricklayers, blacksmiths, and others, who do not get returns from their work as your father does and who cannot send their children to train as primary school teachers because they hardly have enough to eat daily. Such children are already issued with certificates of Bleak Future at about ten years of age. Look at the hospitals. The money that should be used to put medicine there and retain the best doctors has been embezzled and transferred to private bank accounts in Switzerland, to all over Europe and America. Now, tell me, many people die daily in the hospitals due to lack of medicine. They are guilty of murder because their actions lead to several of our people dying untimely deaths. Finished.

Mariama: Well, I'm as passionate as you are, it is the poor person who knows where the pin pinches him or her most, and I do understand what it is to be extremely poor. It is not all the time that woven cloths are profitable or that people have money to buy new clothes. There are times we too do not have dinner at the house and during some big Eid festivals my parents can't buy rams or even afford food at home. And yes, I know these are people who deserve *seriya* as swiftly as possible, but I'm scared of all this violence.

Rafatu: Violence should beget violence.

[*Aafa Layisi walks into the compound. Both Mariama and Rafatu are so absorbed in their dialogue that they do not know that Aafa is listening in on them*]

Mariama: Hun

Rafatu: Emptying Ile-Eni's treasury is violence and no matter how much money thieves spend in a mosque or in bribing the *alafas*, they are still thieves and cannot wash their dirt clean. Finished.

Mariama: You know what [deeply in thought, moving forward to hold Rafatu's hands], come to think of it, emptying of people's treasury is a form of violence on the people. After all, it leads to people dying from hunger and of diseases they should not have died of if there had been medicine and health care facilities at the hospital. I can see your points, Rafatu, we need our laws to reflect this!

Rafatu and Mariama [*holding each other's hands, looking each other in the eyes, simultaneously shaking their heads*] Violence begets violence. Finished.

Aafa Layisi: [*interjecting*]No, it is not finished. There is a matter that can never finish.

Rafatu: [shocked, turns with opened mouth] What? How long have you been eavesdropping on us?
[*Looks at Mariama, who is also shocked, but only gives some smiles*]
What is happening here? Mariama did you see when he came in and you didn't tell me? Whoever knows that it is the red oil that will cook the red pepper! Or that it is water that will cook fish!
[*Hearing Silifatu's voice from her house calling her daughter, listens*]

Can you hear that? I think it's your mom who needs your attention.

Aafa Layisi [*to both ladies as Mariama stands to go*] I enjoyed what I met of your discussion. I didn't want to distract you or stop you from saying your mind. Your wisdom is the Quranic wisdom, turned upside down by our corrupt politicians. Isn't it time we ended our corrupt politicians' dislike of the ordinary man? My Quranic School should not have been opened to the rich politicians as a theatre for their shows. I am at one with all your ideas. Even the little I had disagreed with, I am now your convert. What is a *seriya* if it does not fit the offence! It is an upside-down *seriya* that doesn't fit offence. [*Suddenly focuses his gaze squarely on Rafatu*] Now, finished...[*to both*] That was why I didn't announce my presence. My intention was not to eavesdrop, not at all...[*to Mariama*] Please, give greetings to Silifatu and don't announce my presence to your Dad yet. It is you I have come to see. If you allow it, my parents would come to see your parents soon. In all of my years of Quranic education here in Ile-Eni and of higher Islamic education abroad, in faraway Arab lands where I earned my higher degrees, I have not seen a more articulate woman. You are a true daughter of Ile-Eni, mouth sweeter than salt in speaking words of wisdom. [*Mariama seems as if she would enter the ground. Rafatu pulls her towards Aafa Layisi*] Please answer me.

Rafatu: [*pulling Mariama, and Mariama pulling back, and now facing Aafa Layisi*] Here, when a lady does not reject an honourable proposal, her silence is her expression of saying yes, please Aafa, hurry, go home to your parents! You see, my friend will not say a word. Her silence should be music to your ears. Don't let our parents meet you here...go now...it is the man's parents' emissaries that break the news of asking for a woman's hand in marriage.

Aafa Layisi [*smiling profusely with all his face, walking backwards towards the door, his eyes not leaving Mariama who has avoided eye contact by all means, burying herself in Rafatu's cover, her heart beating very fast*] You are my happiness, Mariama. We are like moon and sun, both needing each other to touch the world. I thought today I was just organizing *Wolima* for my students not knowing it was the eve of the bigger ceremony for myself. A unity of sun and moon to bring forth little lights to the world: little lights are salts of the world! *Omo ni iyo aye*[10], as our people say!
[*As Aafa Layisi goes eagerly away, Mariama and Rafatu run to Mariama's mother, all excitement in their faces*]

Mariama: [*running towards the inner house, Rafatu following*] Mama where are you? Mama! Mama! Mama!

Rafatu: [*running with visible excitement after her friend, making a jest of Mariama and beckoning her as if telling her to slow down her run with which she also indicates*

---

[10] Yoruba saying that "children are salt of the World"

her own excitement] *Iyawo yeye! Iyawo yeye!* The back of the wife will not labour for long on the bed!

The End

Glossary

Alaafa, a Muslim cleric

Alubarika, [God's] blessings

Amala, mashed food made from yam flower.

Aasitu! Aassituu lillahi!, a plead: "Quiet, quiet for the sake of God!"

Bembe, a musical drum, also used to call the music produced by the drum

Ehoro, Rabbit

Ejo, Snake

Elaloro, a call for analysis, explanation and interpretation

Gafara, used to mean "excuse me" or just to ask for permission to enter a house, or place of any kind.

Gbajumo, Elite, famous, popular

Irú, locust bean

Jumaa salat, Friday prayers, offered as a special prayer different from the five daily prayer, often used to replace the afternoon one from the five

Magaji, head of a compound or village

Okuku, a small wooden cart carrying the spread wood being weaved by a weaver and being pulled along towards him or her

Salat, Muslim ritual prayers, obligatorily done five times a day, also non-obligatory ones there-apart

Wolima, ceremony marking the completion of portions of, or the entire Quran

Printed in the United States
By Bookmasters